This journal belongs to

Book	
Author	
Publisher	

Genre		Pages	
My Rating ☆☆☆☆☆		Fiction ☐ Non-Fiction ☐	

Date Started	Date Finished

Summary

Favorite Quotes	Would I Recommend?

Book	
Author	
Publisher	

Genre	Pages
My Rating ☆☆☆☆☆	Fiction ☐ Non-Fiction ☐
Date Started	Date Finished

Summary

Favorite Quotes	Would I Recommend?

Book	
Author	
Publisher	

Genre		Pages	
My Rating	☆ ☆ ☆ ☆ ☆	Fiction ☐ Non-Fiction ☐	

Date Started	Date Finished

Summary

Favorite Quotes	Would I Recommend?

Book	

Author	

Publisher	

Genre	Pages
My Rating ☆ ☆ ☆ ☆ ☆	Fiction □ Non-Fiction □

Date Started	Date Finished

Summary

Favorite Quotes	Would I Recommend?

Book	

Author	

Publisher	

Genre	Pages

My Rating ☆ ☆ ☆ ☆ ☆	Fiction ☐ Non-Fiction ☐

Date Started	Date Finished

Summary

Favorite Quotes	Would I Recommend?

Book	
Author	
Publisher	

Genre		Pages	
My Rating	☆ ☆ ☆ ☆ ☆	Fiction ☐ Non-Fiction ☐	

Date Started		Date Finished	

Summary

Favorite Quotes	Would I Recommend?

Book	
Author	
Publisher	

Genre		Pages	
My Rating ☆ ☆ ☆ ☆ ☆		Fiction □ Non-Fiction □	
Date Started		Date Finished	

Summary

Favorite Quotes	Would I Recommend?

Book	
Author	
Publisher	

Genre	Pages
My Rating ☆ ☆ ☆ ☆ ☆	Fiction ☐ Non-Fiction ☐
Date Started	Date Finished

Summary

Favorite Quotes	Would I Recommend?

Book	
Author	
Publisher	

Genre	Pages
My Rating ☆☆☆☆☆	Fiction □ Non-Fiction □
Date Started	Date Finished

Summary

Favorite Quotes	Would I Recommend?

Book	

Author	

Publisher	

Genre	Pages

My Rating ☆ ☆ ☆ ☆ ☆	Fiction ☐ Non-Fiction ☐

Date Started	Date Finished

Summary

Favorite Quotes	Would I Recommend?

Book	
Author	
Publisher	

Genre	Pages
My Rating ☆☆☆☆☆	Fiction □ Non-Fiction □

Date Started	Date Finished

Summary

Favorite Quotes	Would I Recommend?

Book	

Author	

Publisher	

Genre		Pages	
My Rating	☆ ☆ ☆ ☆ ☆	Fiction ☐ Non-Fiction ☐	
Date Started		Date Finished	

Summary

Favorite Quotes	Would I Recommend?

Book	
Author	
Publisher	

Genre		Pages	
My Rating	☆☆☆☆☆	Fiction ☐ Non-Fiction ☐	

Date Started	Date Finished

Summary

Favorite Quotes	Would I Recommend?

Book	
Author	
Publisher	

Genre		Pages	
My Rating	☆☆☆☆☆	Fiction ☐ Non-Fiction ☐	

Date Started	Date Finished

Summary

Favorite Quotes	Would I Recommend?

Book	
Author	
Publisher	

Genre	Pages
My Rating ☆ ☆ ☆ ☆ ☆	Fiction ☐ Non-Fiction ☐
Date Started	Date Finished

Summary

Favorite Quotes	Would I Recommend?

Book	
Author	
Publisher	

Genre		Pages	
My Rating ☆ ☆ ☆ ☆ ☆		Fiction ☐ Non-Fiction ☐	
Date Started		Date Finished	

Summary

Favorite Quotes	Would I Recommend?

Book	
Author	
Publisher	

Genre	Pages
My Rating ☆ ☆ ☆ ☆ ☆	Fiction ☐ Non-Fiction ☐

Date Started	Date Finished

Summary

Favorite Quotes	Would I Recommend?

Book	
Author	
Publisher	

Genre	Pages
My Rating ☆☆☆☆☆	Fiction ☐ Non-Fiction ☐

Date Started	Date Finished

Summary

Favorite Quotes	Would I Recommend?

Book	
Author	
Publisher	

Genre	Pages
My Rating ☆ ☆ ☆ ☆ ☆	Fiction ☐ Non-Fiction ☐
Date Started	Date Finished

Summary

Favorite Quotes	Would I Recommend?

Book	
Author	
Publisher	

Genre		Pages	
My Rating	☆ ☆ ☆ ☆ ☆	Fiction ☐ Non-Fiction ☐
Date Started		Date Finished	

Summary

Favorite Quotes	Would I Recommend?

Book	
Author	
Publisher	

Genre		Pages
My Rating ☆☆☆☆☆		Fiction ☐ Non-Fiction ☐

Date Started	Date Finished

Summary

Favorite Quotes	Would I Recommend?

Book	
Author	
Publisher	

Genre		Pages	
My Rating	☆ ☆ ☆ ☆ ☆	Fiction ☐ Non-Fiction ☐
Date Started		Date Finished	

Summary

Favorite Quotes	Would I Recommend?

Book	
Author	
Publisher	

Genre		Pages	
My Rating ☆ ☆ ☆ ☆ ☆		Fiction □ Non-Fiction □	

Date Started	Date Finished

Summary

Favorite Quotes	Would I Recommend?

Book	
Author	
Publisher	

Genre	Pages
My Rating ☆☆☆☆☆	Fiction ☐ Non-Fiction ☐

Date Started	Date Finished

Summary

Favorite Quotes	Would I Recommend?

Book	
Author	
Publisher	

Genre		Pages
My Rating ☆☆☆☆☆		Fiction ☐ Non-Fiction ☐

Date Started	Date Finished

Summary

Favorite Quotes	Would I Recommend?

Book	
Author	
Publisher	

Genre	Pages
My Rating ☆ ☆ ☆ ☆ ☆	Fiction ☐ Non-Fiction ☐
Date Started	Date Finished

Summary

Favorite Quotes	Would I Recommend?

Book	
Author	
Publisher	

Genre		Pages
My Rating ☆ ☆ ☆ ☆ ☆		Fiction ☐ Non-Fiction ☐

Date Started	Date Finished

Summary

Favorite Quotes	Would I Recommend?

Book	
Author	
Publisher	

Genre	Pages
My Rating ☆ ☆ ☆ ☆ ☆	Fiction ☐ Non-Fiction ☐

Date Started	Date Finished

Summary

Favorite Quotes	Would I Recommend?

Book	
Author	
Publisher	

Genre		Pages	
My Rating ☆☆☆☆☆		Fiction ☐ Non-Fiction ☐	
Date Started		Date Finished	

Summary

Favorite Quotes	Would I Recommend?

Book	
Author	
Publisher	

Genre	Pages
My Rating ☆☆☆☆☆	Fiction ☐ Non-Fiction ☐

Date Started	Date Finished

Summary

Favorite Quotes	Would I Recommend?

Book	

Author

Publisher

Genre	Pages
My Rating ☆☆☆☆☆	Fiction □ Non-Fiction □

Date Started	Date Finished

Summary

Favorite Quotes	Would I Recommend?

Book	
Author	
Publisher	

Genre		Pages	
My Rating	☆ ☆ ☆ ☆ ☆	Fiction ☐ Non-Fiction ☐	
Date Started		Date Finished	

Summary

Favorite Quotes	Would I Recommend?

Book	
Author	
Publisher	

Genre	Pages
My Rating ☆☆☆☆☆	Fiction ☐ Non-Fiction ☐

Date Started	Date Finished

Summary

Favorite Quotes	Would I Recommend?

Book	
Author	
Publisher	

Genre	Pages
My Rating ☆ ☆ ☆ ☆ ☆	Fiction ☐ Non-Fiction ☐
Date Started	Date Finished

Summary

Favorite Quotes	Would I Recommend?

Book	
Author	
Publisher	

Genre		Pages	
My Rating ☆☆☆☆☆		Fiction ☐ Non-Fiction ☐	

Date Started	Date Finished

Summary

Favorite Quotes	Would I Recommend?

Book	
Author	
Publisher	

Genre		Pages
My Rating	☆ ☆ ☆ ☆ ☆	Fiction ☐ Non-Fiction ☐

Date Started	Date Finished

Summary

Favorite Quotes	Would I Recommend?

Book	
Author	
Publisher	

Genre		Pages	
My Rating ☆☆☆☆☆		Fiction ☐ Non-Fiction ☐	
Date Started		Date Finished	

Summary

Favorite Quotes	Would I Recommend?

Book	
Author	
Publisher	

Genre	Pages
My Rating ☆ ☆ ☆ ☆ ☆	Fiction ☐ Non-Fiction ☐

Date Started	Date Finished

Summary

Favorite Quotes	Would I Recommend?

Book	
Author	
Publisher	

Genre		Pages	
My Rating ☆ ☆ ☆ ☆ ☆		Fiction ☐ Non-Fiction ☐	

Date Started		Date Finished	

Summary

Favorite Quotes	Would I Recommend?

Book	
Author	
Publisher	

Genre		Pages	
My Rating	☆ ☆ ☆ ☆ ☆	Fiction ☐ Non-Fiction ☐	

Date Started		Date Finished	

Summary

Favorite Quotes	Would I Recommend?

Book	
Author	
Publisher	

Genre	Pages
My Rating ☆☆☆☆☆	Fiction ☐ Non-Fiction ☐
Date Started	Date Finished

Summary

Favorite Quotes	Would I Recommend?

Book	
Author	
Publisher	

Genre	Pages
My Rating ☆☆☆☆☆	Fiction ☐ Non-Fiction ☐

Date Started	Date Finished

Summary

Favorite Quotes	Would I Recommend?

Book	
Author	
Publisher	

Genre		Pages	
My Rating ☆☆☆☆☆		Fiction ☐ Non-Fiction ☐	
Date Started		Date Finished	

Summary

Favorite Quotes	Would I Recommend?

Book	
Author	
Publisher	

Genre	Pages
My Rating ☆ ☆ ☆ ☆ ☆	Fiction ☐ Non-Fiction ☐
Date Started	Date Finished

Summary

Favorite Quotes	Would I Recommend?

Book	
Author	
Publisher	

Genre		Pages	
My Rating	☆ ☆ ☆ ☆ ☆	Fiction □ Non-Fiction □	
Date Started		Date Finished	

Summary

Favorite Quotes	Would I Recommend?

Book	
Author	
Publisher	

Genre	Pages
My Rating ☆☆☆☆☆	Fiction ☐ Non-Fiction ☐

Date Started	Date Finished

Summary

Favorite Quotes	Would I Recommend?

Book	
Author	
Publisher	

Genre	Pages
My Rating ☆ ☆ ☆ ☆ ☆	Fiction ☐ Non-Fiction ☐
Date Started	Date Finished

Summary

Favorite Quotes	Would I Recommend?

Book	

Author	

Publisher	

Genre	Pages

My Rating ☆☆☆☆☆	Fiction ☐ Non-Fiction ☐

Date Started	Date Finished

Summary

Favorite Quotes	Would I Recommend?

Book	

Author	

Publisher	

Genre		Pages	
My Rating	☆ ☆ ☆ ☆ ☆	Fiction ☐ Non-Fiction ☐	

Date Started	Date Finished

Summary

Favorite Quotes	Would I Recommend?

Book	
Author	
Publisher	

Genre	Pages
My Rating ☆☆☆☆☆	Fiction ☐ Non-Fiction ☐

Date Started	Date Finished

Summary

Favorite Quotes	Would I Recommend?

Book	
Author	
Publisher	

Genre		Pages	
My Rating ☆ ☆ ☆ ☆ ☆		Fiction ☐ Non-Fiction ☐	

Date Started	Date Finished

Summary

Favorite Quotes	Would I Recommend?

Book	
Author	
Publisher	

Genre	Pages
My Rating ☆ ☆ ☆ ☆ ☆	Fiction ☐ Non-Fiction ☐
Date Started	Date Finished

Summary

Favorite Quotes	Would I Recommend?

Book	
Author	
Publisher	

Genre	Pages
My Rating ☆ ☆ ☆ ☆ ☆	Fiction ☐ Non-Fiction ☐
Date Started	Date Finished

Summary

Favorite Quotes	Would I Recommend?

Book	

Author	

Publisher	

Genre	Pages

My Rating ☆☆☆☆☆	Fiction ☐ Non-Fiction ☐

Date Started	Date Finished

Summary

Favorite Quotes	Would I Recommend?

Book	
Author	
Publisher	

Genre		Pages	
My Rating ☆☆☆☆☆		Fiction □ Non-Fiction □	
Date Started		Date Finished	

Summary

Favorite Quotes	Would I Recommend?

Book	
Author	
Publisher	

Genre	Pages
My Rating ☆☆☆☆☆	Fiction ☐ Non-Fiction ☐

Date Started	Date Finished

Summary

Favorite Quotes	Would I Recommend?

Book	
Author	
Publisher	

Genre		Pages	
My Rating ☆☆☆☆☆		Fiction ☐ Non-Fiction ☐	

Date Started	Date Finished

Summary

Favorite Quotes	Would I Recommend?

Book	
Author	
Publisher	

Genre	Pages
My Rating ☆ ☆ ☆ ☆ ☆	Fiction □ Non-Fiction □

Date Started	Date Finished

Summary

Favorite Quotes	Would I Recommend?

Book	
Author	
Publisher	

Genre	Pages
My Rating ☆ ☆ ☆ ☆ ☆	Fiction □ Non-Fiction □

Date Started	Date Finished

Summary

Favorite Quotes	Would I Recommend?

Book	
Author	
Publisher	

Genre		Pages	
My Rating	☆ ☆ ☆ ☆ ☆	Fiction ☐ Non-Fiction ☐	

Date Started	Date Finished

Summary

Favorite Quotes	Would I Recommend?

Book	

Author	

Publisher	

Genre		Pages	
My Rating ☆ ☆ ☆ ☆ ☆		Fiction □ Non-Fiction □	
Date Started		Date Finished	

Summary

Favorite Quotes	Would I Recommend?

Book	
Author	
Publisher	

Genre	Pages
My Rating ☆ ☆ ☆ ☆ ☆	Fiction □ Non-Fiction □
Date Started	Date Finished

Summary

Favorite Quotes	Would I Recommend?

Book	
Author	
Publisher	

Genre		Pages
My Rating ☆ ☆ ☆ ☆ ☆		Fiction ☐ Non-Fiction ☐

Date Started	Date Finished

Summary

Favorite Quotes	Would I Recommend?

Book	
Author	
Publisher	

Genre		Pages	
My Rating	☆ ☆ ☆ ☆ ☆	Fiction □ Non-Fiction □

Date Started		Date Finished

Summary

Favorite Quotes	Would I Recommend?

Book	
Author	
Publisher	

Genre		Pages
My Rating ☆☆☆☆☆		Fiction ☐ Non-Fiction ☐

Date Started	Date Finished

Summary

Favorite Quotes	Would I Recommend?

Book	
Author	
Publisher	

Genre		Pages	
My Rating	☆ ☆ ☆ ☆ ☆	Fiction ☐ Non-Fiction ☐	

Date Started	Date Finished

Summary

Favorite Quotes	Would I Recommend?

Book	
Author	
Publisher	

Genre		Pages
My Rating ☆☆☆☆☆		Fiction ☐ Non-Fiction ☐

Date Started	Date Finished

Summary

Favorite Quotes	Would I Recommend?

Book	
Author	
Publisher	

Genre	Pages
My Rating ☆☆☆☆☆	Fiction ☐ Non-Fiction ☐

Date Started	Date Finished

Summary

Favorite Quotes	Would I Recommend?

Book	
Author	
Publisher	

Genre	Pages
My Rating ☆☆☆☆☆	Fiction ☐ Non-Fiction ☐

Date Started	Date Finished

Summary

Favorite Quotes	Would I Recommend?

Book	
Author	
Publisher	

Genre	Pages
My Rating ☆ ☆ ☆ ☆ ☆	Fiction ☐ Non-Fiction ☐

Date Started	Date Finished

Summary

Favorite Quotes	Would I Recommend?

Book	
Author	
Publisher	

Genre	Pages
My Rating ☆☆☆☆☆	Fiction ☐ Non-Fiction ☐
Date Started	Date Finished

Summary

Favorite Quotes	Would I Recommend?

Book	
Author	
Publisher	

Genre	Pages
My Rating ☆☆☆☆☆	Fiction ☐ Non-Fiction ☐

Date Started	Date Finished

Summary

Favorite Quotes	Would I Recommend?

Book	
Author	
Publisher	

Genre		Pages	
My Rating	☆ ☆ ☆ ☆ ☆	Fiction ☐ Non-Fiction ☐

Date Started	Date Finished

Summary

Favorite Quotes	Would I Recommend?

Book	

Author	

Publisher	

Genre	Pages

My Rating ☆ ☆ ☆ ☆ ☆	Fiction ☐ Non-Fiction ☐

Date Started	Date Finished

Summary

Favorite Quotes	Would I Recommend?

Book	

Author

Publisher

Genre	Pages
My Rating ☆☆☆☆☆	Fiction ☐ Non-Fiction ☐

Date Started	Date Finished

Summary

Favorite Quotes	Would I Recommend?

Book	
Author	
Publisher	

Genre	Pages
My Rating ☆☆☆☆☆	Fiction ☐ Non-Fiction ☐

Date Started	Date Finished

Summary

Favorite Quotes	Would I Recommend?

Book	
Author	
Publisher	

Genre		Pages	
My Rating ☆ ☆ ☆ ☆ ☆		Fiction ☐ Non-Fiction ☐	

Date Started	Date Finished

Summary

Favorite Quotes	Would I Recommend?

Book

Author

Publisher

Genre	Pages
My Rating ☆ ☆ ☆ ☆ ☆	Fiction ☐ Non-Fiction ☐

Date Started	Date Finished

Summary

Favorite Quotes	Would I Recommend?

Book	

Author	

Publisher	

Genre		Pages	

My Rating	☆ ☆ ☆ ☆ ☆	Fiction ☐ Non-Fiction ☐

Date Started		Date Finished	

Summary

Favorite Quotes	Would I Recommend?

BOOK		READ?
	Fiction □ Non-Fiction □	
	Fiction □ Non-Fiction □	
	Fiction □ Non-Fiction □	
	Fiction □ Non-Fiction □	
	Fiction □ Non-Fiction □	
	Fiction □ Non-Fiction □	
	Fiction □ Non-Fiction □	
	Fiction □ Non-Fiction □	
	Fiction □ Non-Fiction □	
	Fiction □ Non-Fiction □	
	Fiction □ Non-Fiction □	
	Fiction □ Non-Fiction □	
	Fiction □ Non-Fiction □	
	Fiction □ Non-Fiction □	
	Fiction □ Non-Fiction □	
	Fiction □ Non-Fiction □	
	Fiction □ Non-Fiction □	
	Fiction □ Non-Fiction □	
	Fiction □ Non-Fiction □	

BOOK		READ?
	Fiction □ Non-Fiction □	
	Fiction □ Non-Fiction □	
	Fiction □ Non-Fiction □	
	Fiction □ Non-Fiction □	
	Fiction □ Non-Fiction □	
	Fiction □ Non-Fiction □	
	Fiction □ Non-Fiction □	
	Fiction □ Non-Fiction □	
	Fiction □ Non-Fiction □	
	Fiction □ Non-Fiction □	
	Fiction □ Non-Fiction □	
	Fiction □ Non-Fiction □	
	Fiction □ Non-Fiction □	
	Fiction □ Non-Fiction □	
	Fiction □ Non-Fiction □	
	Fiction □ Non-Fiction □	
	Fiction □ Non-Fiction □	
	Fiction □ Non-Fiction □	
	Fiction □ Non-Fiction □	

BOOKS TO READ

BOOK		READ?
	Fiction ☐ Non-Fiction ☐	
	Fiction ☐ Non-Fiction ☐	
	Fiction ☐ Non-Fiction ☐	
	Fiction ☐ Non-Fiction ☐	
	Fiction ☐ Non-Fiction ☐	
	Fiction ☐ Non-Fiction ☐	
	Fiction ☐ Non-Fiction ☐	
	Fiction ☐ Non-Fiction ☐	
	Fiction ☐ Non-Fiction ☐	
	Fiction ☐ Non-Fiction ☐	
	Fiction ☐ Non-Fiction ☐	
	Fiction ☐ Non-Fiction ☐	
	Fiction ☐ Non-Fiction ☐	
	Fiction ☐ Non-Fiction ☐	
	Fiction ☐ Non-Fiction ☐	
	Fiction ☐ Non-Fiction ☐	
	Fiction ☐ Non-Fiction ☐	
	Fiction ☐ Non-Fiction ☐	
	Fiction ☐ Non-Fiction ☐	

BOOK		READ?
	Fiction □ Non-Fiction □	
	Fiction □ Non-Fiction □	
	Fiction □ Non-Fiction □	
	Fiction □ Non-Fiction □	
	Fiction □ Non-Fiction □	
	Fiction □ Non-Fiction □	
	Fiction □ Non-Fiction □	
	Fiction □ Non-Fiction □	
	Fiction □ Non-Fiction □	
	Fiction □ Non-Fiction □	
	Fiction □ Non-Fiction □	
	Fiction □ Non-Fiction □	
	Fiction □ Non-Fiction □	
	Fiction □ Non-Fiction □	
	Fiction □ Non-Fiction □	
	Fiction □ Non-Fiction □	
	Fiction □ Non-Fiction □	
	Fiction □ Non-Fiction □	
	Fiction □ Non-Fiction □	

BOOK		READ?
	Fiction □ Non-Fiction □	
	Fiction □ Non-Fiction □	
	Fiction □ Non-Fiction □	
	Fiction □ Non-Fiction □	
	Fiction □ Non-Fiction □	
	Fiction □ Non-Fiction □	
	Fiction □ Non-Fiction □	
	Fiction □ Non-Fiction □	
	Fiction □ Non-Fiction □	
	Fiction □ Non-Fiction □	
	Fiction □ Non-Fiction □	
	Fiction □ Non-Fiction □	
	Fiction □ Non-Fiction □	
	Fiction □ Non-Fiction □	
	Fiction □ Non-Fiction □	
	Fiction □ Non-Fiction □	
	Fiction □ Non-Fiction □	
	Fiction □ Non-Fiction □	
	Fiction □ Non-Fiction □	

BOOKS TO READ

BOOK		READ?
	Fiction □ Non-Fiction □	
	Fiction □ Non-Fiction □	
	Fiction □ Non-Fiction □	
	Fiction □ Non-Fiction □	
	Fiction □ Non-Fiction □	
	Fiction □ Non-Fiction □	
	Fiction □ Non-Fiction □	
	Fiction □ Non-Fiction □	
	Fiction □ Non-Fiction □	
	Fiction □ Non-Fiction □	
	Fiction □ Non-Fiction □	
	Fiction □ Non-Fiction □	
	Fiction □ Non-Fiction □	
	Fiction □ Non-Fiction □	
	Fiction □ Non-Fiction □	
	Fiction □ Non-Fiction □	
	Fiction □ Non-Fiction □	
	Fiction □ Non-Fiction □	
	Fiction □ Non-Fiction □	

BOOKS TO READ

BOOK		READ?
	Fiction □ Non-Fiction □	
	Fiction □ Non-Fiction □	
	Fiction □ Non-Fiction □	
	Fiction □ Non-Fiction □	
	Fiction □ Non-Fiction □	
	Fiction □ Non-Fiction □	
	Fiction □ Non-Fiction □	
	Fiction □ Non-Fiction □	
	Fiction □ Non-Fiction □	
	Fiction □ Non-Fiction □	
	Fiction □ Non-Fiction □	
	Fiction □ Non-Fiction □	
	Fiction □ Non-Fiction □	
	Fiction □ Non-Fiction □	
	Fiction □ Non-Fiction □	
	Fiction □ Non-Fiction □	
	Fiction □ Non-Fiction □	
	Fiction □ Non-Fiction □	
	Fiction □ Non-Fiction □	
	Fiction □ Non-Fiction □	

BOOKS TO READ

BOOK		READ?
	Fiction □ Non-Fiction □	
	Fiction □ Non-Fiction □	
	Fiction □ Non-Fiction □	
	Fiction □ Non-Fiction □	
	Fiction □ Non-Fiction □	
	Fiction □ Non-Fiction □	
	Fiction □ Non-Fiction □	
	Fiction □ Non-Fiction □	
	Fiction □ Non-Fiction □	
	Fiction □ Non-Fiction □	
	Fiction □ Non-Fiction □	
	Fiction □ Non-Fiction □	
	Fiction □ Non-Fiction □	
	Fiction □ Non-Fiction □	
	Fiction □ Non-Fiction □	
	Fiction □ Non-Fiction □	
	Fiction □ Non-Fiction □	
	Fiction □ Non-Fiction □	
	Fiction □ Non-Fiction □	

BOOK		READ?
	Fiction □ Non-Fiction □	
	Fiction □ Non-Fiction □	
	Fiction □ Non-Fiction □	
	Fiction □ Non-Fiction □	
	Fiction □ Non-Fiction □	
	Fiction □ Non-Fiction □	
	Fiction □ Non-Fiction □	
	Fiction □ Non-Fiction □	
	Fiction □ Non-Fiction □	
	Fiction □ Non-Fiction □	
	Fiction □ Non-Fiction □	
	Fiction □ Non-Fiction □	
	Fiction □ Non-Fiction □	
	Fiction □ Non-Fiction □	
	Fiction □ Non-Fiction □	
	Fiction □ Non-Fiction □	
	Fiction □ Non-Fiction □	
	Fiction □ Non-Fiction □	
	Fiction □ Non-Fiction □	
	Fiction □ Non-Fiction □	

BOOKS TO READ

BOOK		READ?
	Fiction □ Non-Fiction □	
	Fiction □ Non-Fiction □	
	Fiction □ Non-Fiction □	
	Fiction □ Non-Fiction □	
	Fiction □ Non-Fiction □	
	Fiction □ Non-Fiction □	
	Fiction □ Non-Fiction □	
	Fiction □ Non-Fiction □	
	Fiction □ Non-Fiction □	
	Fiction □ Non-Fiction □	
	Fiction □ Non-Fiction □	
	Fiction □ Non-Fiction □	
	Fiction □ Non-Fiction □	
	Fiction □ Non-Fiction □	
	Fiction □ Non-Fiction □	
	Fiction □ Non-Fiction □	
	Fiction □ Non-Fiction □	
	Fiction □ Non-Fiction □	
	Fiction □ Non-Fiction □	
	Fiction □ Non-Fiction □	

BOOK		READ?
	Fiction ☐ Non-Fiction ☐	
	Fiction ☐ Non-Fiction ☐	
	Fiction ☐ Non-Fiction ☐	
	Fiction ☐ Non-Fiction ☐	
	Fiction ☐ Non-Fiction ☐	
	Fiction ☐ Non-Fiction ☐	
	Fiction ☐ Non-Fiction ☐	
	Fiction ☐ Non-Fiction ☐	
	Fiction ☐ Non-Fiction ☐	
	Fiction ☐ Non-Fiction ☐	
	Fiction ☐ Non-Fiction ☐	
	Fiction ☐ Non-Fiction ☐	
	Fiction ☐ Non-Fiction ☐	
	Fiction ☐ Non-Fiction ☐	
	Fiction ☐ Non-Fiction ☐	
	Fiction ☐ Non-Fiction ☐	
	Fiction ☐ Non-Fiction ☐	
	Fiction ☐ Non-Fiction ☐	

BOOK		READ?
	Fiction ☐ Non-Fiction ☐	
	Fiction ☐ Non-Fiction ☐	
	Fiction ☐ Non-Fiction ☐	
	Fiction ☐ Non-Fiction ☐	
	Fiction ☐ Non-Fiction ☐	
	Fiction ☐ Non-Fiction ☐	
	Fiction ☐ Non-Fiction ☐	
	Fiction ☐ Non-Fiction ☐	
	Fiction ☐ Non-Fiction ☐	
	Fiction ☐ Non-Fiction ☐	
	Fiction ☐ Non-Fiction ☐	
	Fiction ☐ Non-Fiction ☐	
	Fiction ☐ Non-Fiction ☐	
	Fiction ☐ Non-Fiction ☐	
	Fiction ☐ Non-Fiction ☐	
	Fiction ☐ Non-Fiction ☐	
	Fiction ☐ Non-Fiction ☐	
	Fiction ☐ Non-Fiction ☐	
	Fiction ☐ Non-Fiction ☐	
	Fiction ☐ Non-Fiction ☐	

BOOKS TO READ

BOOK		READ?
	Fiction □ Non-Fiction □	
	Fiction □ Non-Fiction □	
	Fiction □ Non-Fiction □	
	Fiction □ Non-Fiction □	
	Fiction □ Non-Fiction □	
	Fiction □ Non-Fiction □	
	Fiction □ Non-Fiction □	
	Fiction □ Non-Fiction □	
	Fiction □ Non-Fiction □	
	Fiction □ Non-Fiction □	
	Fiction □ Non-Fiction □	
	Fiction □ Non-Fiction □	
	Fiction □ Non-Fiction □	
	Fiction □ Non-Fiction □	
	Fiction □ Non-Fiction □	
	Fiction □ Non-Fiction □	
	Fiction □ Non-Fiction □	
	Fiction □ Non-Fiction □	
	Fiction □ Non-Fiction □	
	Fiction □ Non-Fiction □	

BOOKS TO READ

BOOK		READ?
	Fiction □ Non-Fiction □	
	Fiction □ Non-Fiction □	
	Fiction □ Non-Fiction □	
	Fiction □ Non-Fiction □	
	Fiction □ Non-Fiction □	
	Fiction □ Non-Fiction □	
	Fiction □ Non-Fiction □	
	Fiction □ Non-Fiction □	
	Fiction □ Non-Fiction □	
	Fiction □ Non-Fiction □	
	Fiction □ Non-Fiction □	
	Fiction □ Non-Fiction □	
	Fiction □ Non-Fiction □	
	Fiction □ Non-Fiction □	
	Fiction □ Non-Fiction □	
	Fiction □ Non-Fiction □	
	Fiction □ Non-Fiction □	
	Fiction □ Non-Fiction □	
	Fiction □ Non-Fiction □	

BOOK		READ?
	Fiction ☐ Non-Fiction ☐	
	Fiction ☐ Non-Fiction ☐	
	Fiction ☐ Non-Fiction ☐	
	Fiction ☐ Non-Fiction ☐	
	Fiction ☐ Non-Fiction ☐	
	Fiction ☐ Non-Fiction ☐	
	Fiction ☐ Non-Fiction ☐	
	Fiction ☐ Non-Fiction ☐	
	Fiction ☐ Non-Fiction ☐	
	Fiction ☐ Non-Fiction ☐	
	Fiction ☐ Non-Fiction ☐	
	Fiction ☐ Non-Fiction ☐	
	Fiction ☐ Non-Fiction ☐	
	Fiction ☐ Non-Fiction ☐	
	Fiction ☐ Non-Fiction ☐	
	Fiction ☐ Non-Fiction ☐	
	Fiction ☐ Non-Fiction ☐	
	Fiction ☐ Non-Fiction ☐	
	Fiction ☐ Non-Fiction ☐	

BOOKS TO READ

BOOK   READ?

	Fiction ☐ Non-Fiction ☐	
	Fiction ☐ Non-Fiction ☐	
	Fiction ☐ Non-Fiction ☐	
	Fiction ☐ Non-Fiction ☐	
	Fiction ☐ Non-Fiction ☐	
	Fiction ☐ Non-Fiction ☐	
	Fiction ☐ Non-Fiction ☐	
	Fiction ☐ Non-Fiction ☐	
	Fiction ☐ Non-Fiction ☐	
	Fiction ☐ Non-Fiction ☐	
	Fiction ☐ Non-Fiction ☐	
	Fiction ☐ Non-Fiction ☐	
	Fiction ☐ Non-Fiction ☐	
	Fiction ☐ Non-Fiction ☐	
	Fiction ☐ Non-Fiction ☐	
	Fiction ☐ Non-Fiction ☐	
	Fiction ☐ Non-Fiction ☐	
	Fiction ☐ Non-Fiction ☐	
	Fiction ☐ Non-Fiction ☐	
	Fiction ☐ Non-Fiction ☐	

BOOKS TO READ

BOOK		READ?
	Fiction □ Non-Fiction □	
	Fiction □ Non-Fiction □	
	Fiction □ Non-Fiction □	
	Fiction □ Non-Fiction □	
	Fiction □ Non-Fiction □	
	Fiction □ Non-Fiction □	
	Fiction □ Non-Fiction □	
	Fiction □ Non-Fiction □	
	Fiction □ Non-Fiction □	
	Fiction □ Non-Fiction □	
	Fiction □ Non-Fiction □	
	Fiction □ Non-Fiction □	
	Fiction □ Non-Fiction □	
	Fiction □ Non-Fiction □	
	Fiction □ Non-Fiction □	
	Fiction □ Non-Fiction □	
	Fiction □ Non-Fiction □	
	Fiction □ Non-Fiction □	
	Fiction □ Non-Fiction □	
	Fiction □ Non-Fiction □	

BOOKS TO READ

BOOK		READ?
	Fiction ☐ Non-Fiction ☐	
	Fiction ☐ Non-Fiction ☐	
	Fiction ☐ Non-Fiction ☐	
	Fiction ☐ Non-Fiction ☐	
	Fiction ☐ Non-Fiction ☐	
	Fiction ☐ Non-Fiction ☐	
	Fiction ☐ Non-Fiction ☐	
	Fiction ☐ Non-Fiction ☐	
	Fiction ☐ Non-Fiction ☐	
	Fiction ☐ Non-Fiction ☐	
	Fiction ☐ Non-Fiction ☐	
	Fiction ☐ Non-Fiction ☐	
	Fiction ☐ Non-Fiction ☐	
	Fiction ☐ Non-Fiction ☐	
	Fiction ☐ Non-Fiction ☐	
	Fiction ☐ Non-Fiction ☐	
	Fiction ☐ Non-Fiction ☐	
	Fiction ☐ Non-Fiction ☐	
	Fiction ☐ Non-Fiction ☐	

BOOKS TO READ

BOOK		READ?
	Fiction □ Non-Fiction □	
	Fiction □ Non-Fiction □	
	Fiction □ Non-Fiction □	
	Fiction □ Non-Fiction □	
	Fiction □ Non-Fiction □	
	Fiction □ Non-Fiction □	
	Fiction □ Non-Fiction □	
	Fiction □ Non-Fiction □	
	Fiction □ Non-Fiction □	
	Fiction □ Non-Fiction □	
	Fiction □ Non-Fiction □	
	Fiction □ Non-Fiction □	
	Fiction □ Non-Fiction □	
	Fiction □ Non-Fiction □	
	Fiction □ Non-Fiction □	
	Fiction □ Non-Fiction □	
	Fiction □ Non-Fiction □	
	Fiction □ Non-Fiction □	
	Fiction □ Non-Fiction □	

BOOKS TO READ

BOOK		READ?
	Fiction □ Non-Fiction □	
	Fiction □ Non-Fiction □	
	Fiction □ Non-Fiction □	
	Fiction □ Non-Fiction □	
	Fiction □ Non-Fiction □	
	Fiction □ Non-Fiction □	
	Fiction □ Non-Fiction □	
	Fiction □ Non-Fiction □	
	Fiction □ Non-Fiction □	
	Fiction □ Non-Fiction □	
	Fiction □ Non-Fiction □	
	Fiction □ Non-Fiction □	
	Fiction □ Non-Fiction □	
	Fiction □ Non-Fiction □	
	Fiction □ Non-Fiction □	
	Fiction □ Non-Fiction □	
	Fiction □ Non-Fiction □	
	Fiction □ Non-Fiction □	
	Fiction □ Non-Fiction □	

BOOKS TO READ

BOOK		READ?
	Fiction ☐ Non-Fiction ☐	
	Fiction ☐ Non-Fiction ☐	
	Fiction ☐ Non-Fiction ☐	
	Fiction ☐ Non-Fiction ☐	
	Fiction ☐ Non-Fiction ☐	
	Fiction ☐ Non-Fiction ☐	
	Fiction ☐ Non-Fiction ☐	
	Fiction ☐ Non-Fiction ☐	
	Fiction ☐ Non-Fiction ☐	
	Fiction ☐ Non-Fiction ☐	
	Fiction ☐ Non-Fiction ☐	
	Fiction ☐ Non-Fiction ☐	
	Fiction ☐ Non-Fiction ☐	
	Fiction ☐ Non-Fiction ☐	
	Fiction ☐ Non-Fiction ☐	
	Fiction ☐ Non-Fiction ☐	
	Fiction ☐ Non-Fiction ☐	
	Fiction ☐ Non-Fiction ☐	
	Fiction ☐ Non-Fiction ☐	

BOOKS TO READ

BOOK		READ?
	Fiction □ Non-Fiction □	
	Fiction □ Non-Fiction □	
	Fiction □ Non-Fiction □	
	Fiction □ Non-Fiction □	
	Fiction □ Non-Fiction □	
	Fiction □ Non-Fiction □	
	Fiction □ Non-Fiction □	
	Fiction □ Non-Fiction □	
	Fiction □ Non-Fiction □	
	Fiction □ Non-Fiction □	
	Fiction □ Non-Fiction □	
	Fiction □ Non-Fiction □	
	Fiction □ Non-Fiction □	
	Fiction □ Non-Fiction □	
	Fiction □ Non-Fiction □	
	Fiction □ Non-Fiction □	
	Fiction □ Non-Fiction □	
	Fiction □ Non-Fiction □	
	Fiction □ Non-Fiction □	

BOOKS TO READ

BOOK		READ?
	Fiction □ Non-Fiction □	
	Fiction □ Non-Fiction □	
	Fiction □ Non-Fiction □	
	Fiction □ Non-Fiction □	
	Fiction □ Non-Fiction □	
	Fiction □ Non-Fiction □	
	Fiction □ Non-Fiction □	
	Fiction □ Non-Fiction □	
	Fiction □ Non-Fiction □	
	Fiction □ Non-Fiction □	
	Fiction □ Non-Fiction □	
	Fiction □ Non-Fiction □	
	Fiction □ Non-Fiction □	
	Fiction □ Non-Fiction □	
	Fiction □ Non-Fiction □	
	Fiction □ Non-Fiction □	
	Fiction □ Non-Fiction □	
	Fiction □ Non-Fiction □	
	Fiction □ Non-Fiction □	

BOOKS TO READ

BOOK		READ?
	Fiction □ Non-Fiction □	
	Fiction □ Non-Fiction □	
	Fiction □ Non-Fiction □	
	Fiction □ Non-Fiction □	
	Fiction □ Non-Fiction □	
	Fiction □ Non-Fiction □	
	Fiction □ Non-Fiction □	
	Fiction □ Non-Fiction □	
	Fiction □ Non-Fiction □	
	Fiction □ Non-Fiction □	
	Fiction □ Non-Fiction □	
	Fiction □ Non-Fiction □	
	Fiction □ Non-Fiction □	
	Fiction □ Non-Fiction □	
	Fiction □ Non-Fiction □	
	Fiction □ Non-Fiction □	
	Fiction □ Non-Fiction □	
	Fiction □ Non-Fiction □	
	Fiction □ Non-Fiction □	
	Fiction □ Non-Fiction □	

BOOKS TO READ

BOOK		READ?
	Fiction ☐ Non-Fiction ☐	
	Fiction ☐ Non-Fiction ☐	
	Fiction ☐ Non-Fiction ☐	
	Fiction ☐ Non-Fiction ☐	
	Fiction ☐ Non-Fiction ☐	
	Fiction ☐ Non-Fiction ☐	
	Fiction ☐ Non-Fiction ☐	
	Fiction ☐ Non-Fiction ☐	
	Fiction ☐ Non-Fiction ☐	
	Fiction ☐ Non-Fiction ☐	
	Fiction ☐ Non-Fiction ☐	
	Fiction ☐ Non-Fiction ☐	
	Fiction ☐ Non-Fiction ☐	
	Fiction ☐ Non-Fiction ☐	
	Fiction ☐ Non-Fiction ☐	
	Fiction ☐ Non-Fiction ☐	
	Fiction ☐ Non-Fiction ☐	
	Fiction ☐ Non-Fiction ☐	
	Fiction ☐ Non-Fiction ☐	
	Fiction ☐ Non-Fiction ☐	

BOOKS TO READ

BOOK		READ?
	Fiction □ Non-Fiction □	
	Fiction □ Non-Fiction □	
	Fiction □ Non-Fiction □	
	Fiction □ Non-Fiction □	
	Fiction □ Non-Fiction □	
	Fiction □ Non-Fiction □	
	Fiction □ Non-Fiction □	
	Fiction □ Non-Fiction □	
	Fiction □ Non-Fiction □	
	Fiction □ Non-Fiction □	
	Fiction □ Non-Fiction □	
	Fiction □ Non-Fiction □	
	Fiction □ Non-Fiction □	
	Fiction □ Non-Fiction □	
	Fiction □ Non-Fiction □	
	Fiction □ Non-Fiction □	
	Fiction □ Non-Fiction □	
	Fiction □ Non-Fiction □	

BOOKS TO READ

BOOK		READ?
	Fiction □ Non-Fiction □	
	Fiction □ Non-Fiction □	
	Fiction □ Non-Fiction □	
	Fiction □ Non-Fiction □	
	Fiction □ Non-Fiction □	
	Fiction □ Non-Fiction □	
	Fiction □ Non-Fiction □	
	Fiction □ Non-Fiction □	
	Fiction □ Non-Fiction □	
	Fiction □ Non-Fiction □	
	Fiction □ Non-Fiction □	
	Fiction □ Non-Fiction □	
	Fiction □ Non-Fiction □	
	Fiction □ Non-Fiction □	
	Fiction □ Non-Fiction □	
	Fiction □ Non-Fiction □	
	Fiction □ Non-Fiction □	
	Fiction □ Non-Fiction □	
	Fiction □ Non-Fiction □	

BOOKS TO READ

BOOK		READ?
	Fiction □ Non-Fiction □	
	Fiction □ Non-Fiction □	
	Fiction □ Non-Fiction □	
	Fiction □ Non-Fiction □	
	Fiction □ Non-Fiction □	
	Fiction □ Non-Fiction □	
	Fiction □ Non-Fiction □	
	Fiction □ Non-Fiction □	
	Fiction □ Non-Fiction □	
	Fiction □ Non-Fiction □	
	Fiction □ Non-Fiction □	
	Fiction □ Non-Fiction □	
	Fiction □ Non-Fiction □	
	Fiction □ Non-Fiction □	
	Fiction □ Non-Fiction □	
	Fiction □ Non-Fiction □	
	Fiction □ Non-Fiction □	
	Fiction □ Non-Fiction □	
	Fiction □ Non-Fiction □	

BOOK		READ?
	Fiction □ Non-Fiction □	
	Fiction □ Non-Fiction □	
	Fiction □ Non-Fiction □	
	Fiction □ Non-Fiction □	
	Fiction □ Non-Fiction □	
	Fiction □ Non-Fiction □	
	Fiction □ Non-Fiction □	
	Fiction □ Non-Fiction □	
	Fiction □ Non-Fiction □	
	Fiction □ Non-Fiction □	
	Fiction □ Non-Fiction □	
	Fiction □ Non-Fiction □	
	Fiction □ Non-Fiction □	
	Fiction □ Non-Fiction □	
	Fiction □ Non-Fiction □	
	Fiction □ Non-Fiction □	
	Fiction □ Non-Fiction □	
	Fiction □ Non-Fiction □	
	Fiction □ Non-Fiction □	

BOOKS TO READ

BOOK		READ?
	Fiction □ Non-Fiction □	
	Fiction □ Non-Fiction □	
	Fiction □ Non-Fiction □	
	Fiction □ Non-Fiction □	
	Fiction □ Non-Fiction □	
	Fiction □ Non-Fiction □	
	Fiction □ Non-Fiction □	
	Fiction □ Non-Fiction □	
	Fiction □ Non-Fiction □	
	Fiction □ Non-Fiction □	
	Fiction □ Non-Fiction □	
	Fiction □ Non-Fiction □	
	Fiction □ Non-Fiction □	
	Fiction □ Non-Fiction □	
	Fiction □ Non-Fiction □	
	Fiction □ Non-Fiction □	
	Fiction □ Non-Fiction □	
	Fiction □ Non-Fiction □	
	Fiction □ Non-Fiction □	
	Fiction □ Non-Fiction □	

BOOKS TO READ

BOOK   READ?

BOOK		READ?
	Fiction ☐ Non-Fiction ☐	
	Fiction ☐ Non-Fiction ☐	
	Fiction ☐ Non-Fiction ☐	
	Fiction ☐ Non-Fiction ☐	
	Fiction ☐ Non-Fiction ☐	
	Fiction ☐ Non-Fiction ☐	
	Fiction ☐ Non-Fiction ☐	
	Fiction ☐ Non-Fiction ☐	
	Fiction ☐ Non-Fiction ☐	
	Fiction ☐ Non-Fiction ☐	
	Fiction ☐ Non-Fiction ☐	
	Fiction ☐ Non-Fiction ☐	
	Fiction ☐ Non-Fiction ☐	
	Fiction ☐ Non-Fiction ☐	
	Fiction ☐ Non-Fiction ☐	
	Fiction ☐ Non-Fiction ☐	
	Fiction ☐ Non-Fiction ☐	
	Fiction ☐ Non-Fiction ☐	
	Fiction ☐ Non-Fiction ☐	
	Fiction ☐ Non-Fiction ☐	

BOOKS TO READ

BOOK   READ?

	Fiction □ Non-Fiction □	
	Fiction □ Non-Fiction □	
	Fiction □ Non-Fiction □	
	Fiction □ Non-Fiction □	
	Fiction □ Non-Fiction □	
	Fiction □ Non-Fiction □	
	Fiction □ Non-Fiction □	
	Fiction □ Non-Fiction □	
	Fiction □ Non-Fiction □	
	Fiction □ Non-Fiction □	
	Fiction □ Non-Fiction □	
	Fiction □ Non-Fiction □	
	Fiction □ Non-Fiction □	
	Fiction □ Non-Fiction □	
	Fiction □ Non-Fiction □	
	Fiction □ Non-Fiction □	
	Fiction □ Non-Fiction □	
	Fiction □ Non-Fiction □	
	Fiction □ Non-Fiction □	

BOOKS TO READ

BOOK		READ?
	Fiction □ Non-Fiction □	
	Fiction □ Non-Fiction □	
	Fiction □ Non-Fiction □	
	Fiction □ Non-Fiction □	
	Fiction □ Non-Fiction □	
	Fiction □ Non-Fiction □	
	Fiction □ Non-Fiction □	
	Fiction □ Non-Fiction □	
	Fiction □ Non-Fiction □	
	Fiction □ Non-Fiction □	
	Fiction □ Non-Fiction □	
	Fiction □ Non-Fiction □	
	Fiction □ Non-Fiction □	
	Fiction □ Non-Fiction □	
	Fiction □ Non-Fiction □	
	Fiction □ Non-Fiction □	
	Fiction □ Non-Fiction □	
	Fiction □ Non-Fiction □	
	Fiction □ Non-Fiction □	

BOOK		READ?
	Fiction ☐ Non-Fiction ☐	
	Fiction ☐ Non-Fiction ☐	
	Fiction ☐ Non-Fiction ☐	
	Fiction ☐ Non-Fiction ☐	
	Fiction ☐ Non-Fiction ☐	
	Fiction ☐ Non-Fiction ☐	
	Fiction ☐ Non-Fiction ☐	
	Fiction ☐ Non-Fiction ☐	
	Fiction ☐ Non-Fiction ☐	
	Fiction ☐ Non-Fiction ☐	
	Fiction ☐ Non-Fiction ☐	
	Fiction ☐ Non-Fiction ☐	
	Fiction ☐ Non-Fiction ☐	
	Fiction ☐ Non-Fiction ☐	
	Fiction ☐ Non-Fiction ☐	
	Fiction ☐ Non-Fiction ☐	
	Fiction ☐ Non-Fiction ☐	
	Fiction ☐ Non-Fiction ☐	
	Fiction ☐ Non-Fiction ☐	

BOOK		READ?
	Fiction □ Non-Fiction □	
	Fiction □ Non-Fiction □	
	Fiction □ Non-Fiction □	
	Fiction □ Non-Fiction □	
	Fiction □ Non-Fiction □	
	Fiction □ Non-Fiction □	
	Fiction □ Non-Fiction □	
	Fiction □ Non-Fiction □	
	Fiction □ Non-Fiction □	
	Fiction □ Non-Fiction □	
	Fiction □ Non-Fiction □	
	Fiction □ Non-Fiction □	
	Fiction □ Non-Fiction □	
	Fiction □ Non-Fiction □	
	Fiction □ Non-Fiction □	
	Fiction □ Non-Fiction □	
	Fiction □ Non-Fiction □	
	Fiction □ Non-Fiction □	
	Fiction □ Non-Fiction □	

BOOKS TO READ

BOOK		READ?
	Fiction □ Non-Fiction □	
	Fiction □ Non-Fiction □	
	Fiction □ Non-Fiction □	
	Fiction □ Non-Fiction □	
	Fiction □ Non-Fiction □	
	Fiction □ Non-Fiction □	
	Fiction □ Non-Fiction □	
	Fiction □ Non-Fiction □	
	Fiction □ Non-Fiction □	
	Fiction □ Non-Fiction □	
	Fiction □ Non-Fiction □	
	Fiction □ Non-Fiction □	
	Fiction □ Non-Fiction □	
	Fiction □ Non-Fiction □	
	Fiction □ Non-Fiction □	
	Fiction □ Non-Fiction □	
	Fiction □ Non-Fiction □	
	Fiction □ Non-Fiction □	
	Fiction □ Non-Fiction □	

BOOKS TO READ

BOOK		READ?
	Fiction ☐ Non-Fiction ☐	
	Fiction ☐ Non-Fiction ☐	
	Fiction ☐ Non-Fiction ☐	
	Fiction ☐ Non-Fiction ☐	
	Fiction ☐ Non-Fiction ☐	
	Fiction ☐ Non-Fiction ☐	
	Fiction ☐ Non-Fiction ☐	
	Fiction ☐ Non-Fiction ☐	
	Fiction ☐ Non-Fiction ☐	
	Fiction ☐ Non-Fiction ☐	
	Fiction ☐ Non-Fiction ☐	
	Fiction ☐ Non-Fiction ☐	
	Fiction ☐ Non-Fiction ☐	
	Fiction ☐ Non-Fiction ☐	
	Fiction ☐ Non-Fiction ☐	
	Fiction ☐ Non-Fiction ☐	
	Fiction ☐ Non-Fiction ☐	
	Fiction ☐ Non-Fiction ☐	
	Fiction ☐ Non-Fiction ☐	
	Fiction ☐ Non-Fiction ☐	

BOOKS TO READ

BOOK   READ?

	Fiction ☐ Non-Fiction ☐	
	Fiction ☐ Non-Fiction ☐	
	Fiction ☐ Non-Fiction ☐	
	Fiction ☐ Non-Fiction ☐	
	Fiction ☐ Non-Fiction ☐	
	Fiction ☐ Non-Fiction ☐	
	Fiction ☐ Non-Fiction ☐	
	Fiction ☐ Non-Fiction ☐	
	Fiction ☐ Non-Fiction ☐	
	Fiction ☐ Non-Fiction ☐	
	Fiction ☐ Non-Fiction ☐	
	Fiction ☐ Non-Fiction ☐	
	Fiction ☐ Non-Fiction ☐	
	Fiction ☐ Non-Fiction ☐	
	Fiction ☐ Non-Fiction ☐	
	Fiction ☐ Non-Fiction ☐	
	Fiction ☐ Non-Fiction ☐	
	Fiction ☐ Non-Fiction ☐	
	Fiction ☐ Non-Fiction ☐	

BOOKS TO READ

BOOK		READ?
	Fiction ☐ Non-Fiction ☐	
	Fiction ☐ Non-Fiction ☐	
	Fiction ☐ Non-Fiction ☐	
	Fiction ☐ Non-Fiction ☐	
	Fiction ☐ Non-Fiction ☐	
	Fiction ☐ Non-Fiction ☐	
	Fiction ☐ Non-Fiction ☐	
	Fiction ☐ Non-Fiction ☐	
	Fiction ☐ Non-Fiction ☐	
	Fiction ☐ Non-Fiction ☐	
	Fiction ☐ Non-Fiction ☐	
	Fiction ☐ Non-Fiction ☐	
	Fiction ☐ Non-Fiction ☐	
	Fiction ☐ Non-Fiction ☐	
	Fiction ☐ Non-Fiction ☐	
	Fiction ☐ Non-Fiction ☐	
	Fiction ☐ Non-Fiction ☐	
	Fiction ☐ Non-Fiction ☐	
	Fiction ☐ Non-Fiction ☐	
	Fiction ☐ Non-Fiction ☐	

BOOKS TO READ

BOOK		READ?
	Fiction □ Non-Fiction □	
	Fiction □ Non-Fiction □	
	Fiction □ Non-Fiction □	
	Fiction □ Non-Fiction □	
	Fiction □ Non-Fiction □	
	Fiction □ Non-Fiction □	
	Fiction □ Non-Fiction □	
	Fiction □ Non-Fiction □	
	Fiction □ Non-Fiction □	
	Fiction □ Non-Fiction □	
	Fiction □ Non-Fiction □	
	Fiction □ Non-Fiction □	
	Fiction □ Non-Fiction □	
	Fiction □ Non-Fiction □	
	Fiction □ Non-Fiction □	
	Fiction □ Non-Fiction □	
	Fiction □ Non-Fiction □	
	Fiction □ Non-Fiction □	
	Fiction □ Non-Fiction □	
	Fiction □ Non-Fiction □	

www.ingramcontent.com/pod-product-compliance
Lightning Source LLC
Chambersburg PA
CBHW051430150726
48000CB00005B/2033